EDWIN LUCAS

Divine Expeditions

*A Comprehensive Guide to St. Expedite's Intercession
and Sacred Practices*

Contents

Biography of St. Expedite

St. Expedite, whose name signifies promptness or speed, is a revered saint in the Catholic Church. Though his historical background is veiled in uncertainty, his spiritual influence and the devotion of countless believers have solidified his place among the esteemed saints.

While the precise details of St. Expedite's birth and early life remain unknown, his feast day is celebrated on April 19th. His birth is believed to have taken place in the late 3rd century, and he is revered as the patron saint of urgent causes, rapid resolutions, and swift action.

Descriptions of St. Expedite's physical appearance and attributes differ among various accounts. He is often depicted as a Roman soldier clad in military armor, symbolizing his commitment to the Christian faith and his bravery in the face of persecution. In his hand, he holds a palm branch, representing martyrdom, and a banner bearing the Latin word "HODIE," emphasizing his association with immediacy and the urgency of his aid.

The relics of St. Expedite hold great significance for his devotees. One of the most venerated relics is his head, believed to rest in the church of San Matteo in Mercato, Rome. Throughout the centuries, other fragments of his remains have been enAltard in numerous churches and Altars worldwide, attracting pilgrims seeking solace and divine intervention.

Legend holds that St. Expedite met his martyrdom during the persecution of Christians under the Roman Emperor Diocletian, which took place in the early 4th century. Various accounts describe his death differently, with some claiming he was beheaded, while others suggest crucifixion or other torturous means. Regardless of the precise manner of his martyrdom, St. Expedite's unwavering faith and dedication to Christ in the face of persecution have made him an inspirational figure.

St. Expedite's intercession is renowned for its speed and efficacy. Devotees turn to him in times of pressing need, entrusting their urgent matters to his care and seeking his prompt assistance. His reputation for swiftly answering prayers and granting aid has fostered a strong and loyal following among believers worldwide.

Devotion to St. Expedite has spread across different countries and cultures, with churches and prayer groups dedicated to his honor. The faithful offer prayers, light candles, and express their gratitude for his prompt intervention. Many testimonials attest to the miracles and speedy resolutions attributed to his intercession, further solidifying his place as a beloved and powerful saint.

St. Expedite's life story serves as a testament to the power of faith, the importance of acting promptly, and the significance of seeking divine assistance in times of urgency. His example encourages believers to approach their challenges with courage and to trust in the providence of God, knowing that prompt help can be found through the intercession of St. Expedite.

The devotion to St. Expedite continued to grow throughout

the centuries, and his popularity reached its peak in the 18th and 19th centuries. His cult spread across Europe and the Americas, attracting people from all walks of life who sought his intercession in times of desperation.

The story of St. Expedite's name carries its own intrigue. Some believe that "Expedite" was a title bestowed upon him to signify his swift response to prayers. Others speculate that it may have been derived from the Latin word "expeditus," meaning "unimpeded" or "unobstructed," highlighting his ability to remove obstacles and bring about quick solutions.

While historical documentation about St. Expedite is limited, his spiritual impact is undeniable. Many faithful believers attribute their deliverance from financial struggles, healing from illnesses, reconciliation of relationships, and other urgent needs to his powerful intercession.

The devotion to St. Expedite has transcended denominational boundaries, with individuals from various Christian traditions seeking his aid. Although he is most widely venerated in the Catholic Church, his influence has extended to Orthodox Christians and other Christian denominations who acknowledge his swift assistance in times of crisis.

Today, St. Expedite continues to be celebrated and honored by countless devotees around the world. His feast day on April 19th is marked with special prayers, liturgies, and acts of devotion in churches and Altars dedicated to him. His popularity has also expanded in the digital age, with online communities and social media platforms providing a space for devotees to share their stories and seek support from fellow believers.

The legacy of St. Expedite serves as a reminder that even in the face of adversity and urgency, there is hope and solace to be found through faith and the intercession of saints. His life, though shrouded in mystery, inspires believers to approach their challenges with faith, perseverance, and the belief that timely aid can come from unexpected sources.

Whether seen as a historical figure, a symbol of promptness, or a powerful intercessor, St. Expedite remains an integral part of the lives of many who turn to him in times of need. His unwavering commitment to Christ, his courage in the face of persecution, and his reputation for swift assistance make him a beloved and revered saint, offering hope and solace to those who seek his intercession.

Seeking Divine Intercession: Exploring the Practice of Praying to Saints

Praying to saints has been a longstanding practice within Christianity, with its origins rooted in the early Christian era. This chapter delves into the historical context and development of the veneration of saints, the theological foundations supporting this practice, and the practical implications it holds for believers.

The veneration of saints can be traced back to the early Christian era, particularly during times of persecution. In those challenging times, martyrs stood firm in their faith and willingly sacrificed their lives. They were among the first to be honored as saints, as their courage and devotion served as inspiring examples for other believers. The cult of the saints emerged as a way to honor these martyrs and seek their intercession, recognizing their spiritual connection with God.

Over time, devotion to specific saints grew within local communities. This devotion often arose due to reported miracles associated with their lives or their spiritual significance in addressing particular needs. As Christianity spread, recognition of universal devotions to saints expanded, with saints like St. Peter and St. Paul gaining widespread reverence.

The practice of praying to saints is rooted in the belief in the "**Communion of Saints.**" This concept emphasizes the unity of all believers, both living and deceased, in the Body of Christ. It highlights the spiritual bond that extends beyond earthly life, connecting believers together. Praying to saints is seen as a way to participate in this communion, seeking their intercession as fellow members of the faith.

The practice of praying to saints is based on the understanding that saints, being in the presence of God, can intercede on behalf of believers. This intercession is viewed as a form of mediation, where the saints present the prayers and petitions of individuals to God. It is believed that the saints' close relationship with God grants significance to their intercessory prayers, making them influential advocates on behalf of believers.

Saints are revered as models of virtue and faith, offering inspiration and guidance to believers. By seeking the intercession of saints, believers express their desire to follow in their footsteps and strive to lead lives characterized by holiness and devotion.

Different saints are associated with specific areas of concern or patronages. For example, St. Anthony is known as the patron saint of lost items, and St. Joseph is recognized as the patron saint of workers. Believers may invoke the intercession of a particular saint based on their expertise or connection to specific needs, seeking their aid and support.

Praying to saints deepens one's personal relationship with God, allowing believers to establish a connection with the larger community of faith. This practice fosters a sense of unity and solidarity among believers, both on earth and in heaven, as they engage in a shared spiritual journey.

Praying to saints encourages humility by acknowledging

human dependence on God's grace and the intercession of others. It is an expression of trust in God's providence, recognizing that saints can guide individuals toward God's will and offer assistance in navigating life's challenges.

Bible Supports Praying to the Saints

The majority of "Bible-believing" Christians oppose the Catholic tradition of praying to the saints. These critics are concerned that Catholics would go to hell for offending God by practicing a neo-pagan religion. They have four basic objections of the custom, all of which they strongly advance.

They begin by accusing Catholics of worshiping Mary and the other saints. This is a violation of the first commandment, which states, "You shall not have any other gods before me" (Exodus 20:3). Catholics also make statues of the saints, which violates the following commandment: "You shall not make for yourself an idol or any image which is in the heavens above or on the earth below or in the waters which are under the earth; you shall not bow down and serve them because I am the Lord your God" (Ex. 20:4-5). Catholics create sculptures of the saints they venerate, committing the dual sins of polytheism and idolatry.

The second argument to praying to the saints is that Catholics, even if they do not worship the saints, are summoning the spirits of the dead. Many verses in the Bible expressly ban summoning the dead: "Do not turn to mediums and familiar spirits; do not seek defilement among them" (Lev 19:31). "The soul that turns to mediums and familiar spirits to go whoring after them, I will set my face against that soul and cut him off from the midst of his people" (Lev. 20:6). "The man or woman who becomes a medium or a familiar spirit will surely die; they will cast stones at them; their blood will be on themselves" (Lev. 20:27). "Let not there be found among you anyone who makes his son or daughter pass through the fire, a diviner of divinations, an occultist, a charmer, an enchanter, one who casts spells, or one who questions mediums or familiar spirits, or one who seeks the dead" (Deut. 18:10-11). Because the saints are all dead, no one may counsel them without violating these scriptural commandments.

A third issue is that there is only one mediator between Jesus Christ and the Father. "For there is one God and one Mediator between God and men, a man, Jesus Christ, who has given himself as a ransom for all, the testimony in its own time" (1 Timothy 2:5-6).

As a mediator between sinners and God, Jesus Christ is completely satisfactory. No one should ever seek the intercession of the saints.

The Bible does not instruct Christians to honor the saints, seek their intercession, or maintain their relics, according to a fourth objection. Without a scriptural mandate to do these things, a Christian risks offending God.

The Catholic Church has long preached that a Christian can only worship God, the Father, the Son, and the Holy Spirit. No creature, no matter how nice or beautiful it is no angel, saint, or even the Virgin Mary deserves to be adored. This is the teaching of the creeds (Apostles' Creed: "I believe in one God"; Nicene Creed: "We believe in one God") and the catechisms (Baltimore

Catechism, question 199: "By the first commandment we are commanded to offer to God alone the supreme worship that is due him") and the Church councils (Nicaea, in 325; Rome in 382; Toledo in 675; Lateran IV in 1215; Lyons in 1274; Florence in 1442; Trent from 1545-1563; Vatican I from 1869-1870).

Polytheism and idolatry are both condemned by the Catholic Church. Pope Dionysius criticized the split of one God into three gods, stating that there can only be one God, not three (Letter to Dionysius of Alexandria, A.D. 260). Pope Damasus I forbade the worship of other gods, angels, or archangels, even if God bestowed the title "god" on them in the Bible (Tome of Damasus, confirmed at the Council of Rome, 382).

Apologetic Sermons Against Those Who Reject Sacred Images by John Damascene provides an authoritative description of the Catholic attitude regarding statues and portraits of Mary and the saints: "If we were making images of men and thought them gods and adored them as gods, certainly we would be impious. But we do not do any of these things."

The Baltimore Catechism, question 223, verifies this: "We do not pray to the crucifix or the images and relics of the saints, but to the persons they represent."

Catholic dogma categorically forbids the worship of anyone other than God, as well as the worship of statues of Christ or the saints. What the Church does permit is prayer to the saints for intercession with the one true God. The Church also permits the creation of sculptures to remind people of Christ or a saint: Further, the images of Christ, the Virgin Mother of God, and the other saints are to be kept in reverence in places of worship, and to them due honor and veneration is to be paid-not because it is believed that there is any divinity or power intrinsic to them for which they are revered, nor because it is sought from them, nor that a blind trust is to be attached to images as it was once by the Gentiles who put their hope in idols (Ps. 135:15).

The Council of Trent said in its Session XXV Decree 2 that "it follows that through these images, which we kiss and before which we kneel and uncover our heads, we are adoring Christ and venerating the saints whose likenesses these images bear."

This reflects the mindset of the Old Testament. The Lord instructed the Israelites to "make two cherubim of beaten gold; you will make them for the two ends of the covering [of the Ark of the Covenant]" shortly after giving them the order forbidding the creation of images for worship (Ex. 25:18).

According to the Lord's command, Moses "made the bronze serpent and he set it upon a pole, and it happened that if a serpent bit a man, and he looked to the bronze serpent, he lived" (Num. 21:9). This followed numerous Israelites suffering punishment from snakebite.

The bronze serpent and the gold cherubim were not idols. The bronze serpent served as God's method of curing individuals who had been bitten by deadly snakes, and the cherubim stood in for the angels of God who were present at the Ark of the Covenant. Catholics also erect statues to symbolize the saints' and angels' presence in places like homes and churches.

The Bible declares that trying to communicate with the dead through mediums and seances is a grave sin. The Catholic Church forbids all forms of superstition and summoning the dead since it is a Bible-believing Church (although, of course, it is more than that—the Catholic Church is the only Church to have written the Bible).

The Baltimore Catechism describes the severity of the superstitious sin: "Superstition is by its very nature a mortal sin, but it may be venial either when the matter is slight or when there is a lack of full consent to the act" (question 212).

In no way does the Catholic Church intend for its adherents to engage in superstition when it promotes devotion to and prayer to the saints. The Church never gives its adherents instructions on how to summon the spirits of the dead to engage in conversation. No attempts are made to make them appear, speak messages, tap tables, or do anything similar during seances.

The Church believes that while the saints appear to be dead, they are actually completely alive in Jesus Christ, who is the bread of life and gives life to everyone who eats it (John 6:35, 48, 51, 53–56) and drinks it (John 11:25; 14:6).

Because of the life they have acquired through their faith in Christ Jesus and through partaking of his body and blood, the saints are alive in heaven.

The saints are depicted worshipping God, singing hymns, playing instruments, pleading with Christ to avenge their martyrdom, and praying for the saints on earth in the books of Revelation (Rev. 4:10, 5:8, 6:9-11).

We think that since they are still living, they can speak for us to God. We can believe they will intercede for us in heaven without having to witness their appearance or hear their voices. We have faith that the saints will grant our supplications and bring them to Christ on our behalf.

The Catholic Church has consistently held that Jesus Christ alone can serve as a bridge between God and people. People can only be rescued through Jesus' death and resurrection.

Pope Leo the Great, who held that Jesus Christ had just one nature and not two, issued his Tome against Eutyches in

449. (This was monophysitism's heresy.) One and the same mediator between God and men, Christ Jesus, was both mortal and immortal under different aspects, as was suitable for the alleviation of our distress. This is stated in the Tome, which the Council of Chalcedon accepted as the authentic Catholic teaching on Christ.

As stated in the fifth session of the Council of Trent (1546), "original sin cannot be taken away through the powers of human nature or through a remedy other than the merit of the one mediator, our Lord Jesus Christ, who reconciled us to God in his blood, having become our justice, and sanctification, and redemption."

The one-of-a-kind mediation of Jesus Christ is included as one of these principal mysteries in the Dogmatic Constitution on the Principal Mysteries of the Faith, which was written for the First Vatican Council (1869–1870):

"So, in reality, Christ Jesus is the Mediator between God and Man, One Man Dying for All; He Made Satisfaction to Divine Justice for Us, And He Erased The Handwriting That Was Against Us. He delivered us from our long-standing servitude into the freedom of sons by destroying principalities and powers.

These passages from authoritative Catholic texts demonstrate unequivocally that the Church regards Jesus Christ alone as the only mediator between fallen mankind and the holy God. How does the Church reconcile the notion that we can pray to the saints with this fundamental tenet of the faith?

God demands that we first pray for one another. Both the Old and New Testaments demonstrate this.

God gave King Abimelech the following instructions in a dream: "For [Abraham] is a prophet and he will pray for you, so you shall live" (Genesis 20:7). Let my servant Job pray for you because I will accept his [prayer], lest I make a horror on you, the Lord informs Job's friends when he is furious with them for not speaking appropriately about him (Job 42:8).

In his letter to the Romans, Paul urged them: "I exhort you, brothers, through our Lord Jesus Christ and through the love of the Spirit, to strive with me in prayers to God on my behalf, that I may be delivered from the disobedient in Judaea and that my ministry may be acceptable to the saints in Jerusalem, so that in the joy coming to you through the will of God I may rest with you" (Rom. 15:30–32).

Therefore, confess your sins to one another and pray for one another so that you can receive healing, advises James. According to James 5:16–17, a godly man's prayer has enormous power in its outcomes. Therefore, God commands us to pray for one another, according to the Bible.

This must imply that praying for one another cannot take away from Jesus Christ's function as our exclusive representative before God.

Second, the fact that each individual who is baptized is made a member of the Body of Christ by virtue of the Holy Spirit's action in baptism is the reason that Christians have the ability to pray for one another (1 Cor. 12:11–13). The reason we can pray effectively is because the Christian is a part of Jesus Christ's Body, the Church, and belongs to him.

Because they are still a part of the Body of Christ, we can pray to the saints. Keep in mind that because Christ offers eternal life, every Christian who dies in Him remains an immortal member of His Body. The doctrine behind the Communion of the Saints is this. The Body of Christ includes every member of Christ, both alive and deceased.

This implies that a saint in heaven is still a part of the Body of Christ and is therefore able to pray for other people. Because of their union with Christ and submission to his leadership, the saints' intercession cannot be seen as competing with that of Christ; rather, it is indivisible from Christ's mediation, to him and in whom the saints are united as one body.

Some Christians—indeed, the majority of Protestants—deny that the Bible supports devotion to the saints, but they are mistaken. The Bible exhorts believers to approach the heavenly hosts in the same manner that they approach the Father and Jesus Christ:

But you have come near Mount Zion, the city of the living God, the heavenly Jerusalem, and untold numbers of angels, as well as the congregation and church of the firstborn who have been admitted to heaven, God the judge of all, and the spirits of righteous people who have been made perfect, as well as Jesus, the mediator of a new covenant, and the sprinkled blood that speaks more persuasively than that of Abel (Heb. 12:22–24).

It is evident that the Christian has interacted with a number of heavenly creatures, including God the judge, Jesus the mediator, angels, and the heavenly city of Jerusalem. The term "spirits of righteous ones who have been made perfect" and "the assembly and church of the firstborn who have been enrolled in heaven" can only apply to the saints in heaven.

They are not made of flesh and blood; they are spirits. Second, they are upright individuals who have most likely been made so by Jesus Christ, "who is our righteousness." Thirdly, they are now flawless. Heaven is the only location where the spirits of perfectly good people can reside.

Furthermore, the best way to describe the saints in heaven is as "spirits of righteous ones who have been made perfect." According to this verse, we must approach the heavenly saints in the same way that Christians approach angels, God the judge, Jesus Christ, and his atoning blood.

Does the Bible suggest that we address the saints in prayer? Absolutely, twice. John saw the Lamb, who is Christ Jesus, seated on a throne among four beasts and 24 elders in Revelation 5:8. The 24 elders bowed down before the Lamb in worship as the Lamb took the book with the seven seals, "each one having a harp and golden bowls of incense, which are the prayers of the saints."

Similar events are described in Revelation 8:3–4, where it is stated that the Lamb broke the seventh seal of the book. "Another angel came and stood on the altar, having a golden censer, and many incenses were given to him in order that he would give it with the prayers of all the saints on the golden altar before the throne," says the other angel. Along with the saints' prayers, the smoke of the incense rose before God from the angel's hand.

These verses help us to comprehend how the saints intercede on our behalf. Our prayers are little incense sticks. They have a tasty, pleasant scent. These bits of incense are offered to us by the 24 saintly elders who surround the throne. In front of God's throne, they lit them on fire.

This is a lovely illustration of how the saints' intercession functions. The saints can ignite our prayers with their love and release the power of our prayers because they are so close to the fire of God's love and because they are standing right in front of him.

A Home Altar to St. Expedite

Working With St. Expedite: The Saint of Urgent Matters

I've read about St. Expedite before, but it wasn't until recently that I decided to give him a seat in my house. I set up an altar near the doorway (our primary entrance) and respectfully welcomed his wisdom into our home.

St. Expedite, also known as Saint Expeditus, is a patron saint of urgent matters. He also works against procrastination and delay, helping in times of emergency. St. Expedite loves speed. If you need a solution to a problem immediately, turn to him. People all over the world petition him when they are experiencing financial distress, job hunting, or in relation to legal matters.

He is a "hot way-opening" energy that prefers to be placed by the doorways. The more primary the entrance the better, whether indoors or out — **the front or back door is ideal.** Make sure to keep St. Expedite altars out of any bedroom, his activity is known to cause sleep disturbances. Expedite's feast day is celebrated on April 19.

How to Get Started:

First, you'll need a photo or statue of St. Expedite. You can find statues on eBay, Amazon and any local statue shop. If you would rather start with an image, search for Expedite on Google and find an image you like.

Expedite loves things in threes. Try to set up your started altar for him in a triangle formation. Place the image in the back centered and a red, white or gold candle to the right with a glass of water to the left. This is the simplest setup of an Expedite altar, but not the only way they can be arranged.

Offerings & Altar Items

The two most basic offerings for Expedite as mentioned above is a **candle and glass of water**. However, the bigger and more important your petition, the more you want to offer back to him. If you are asking for something big, you should give the same energy in return when you receive your blessings.

The full list of favored/common Expedite offerings include:

- Candle(s)
- Glass(es) of water
- Slice(s) of pound cake Sarah Lee is rumored to be his favorite, which can be found in the frozen desserts section of many grocery stores, but homemade or other brands will no doubt suffice.
- Red flowers, especially roses

- Red wine
- Palm fronds

You do not have to give all of these at once. I**t actually works better to "pay" St. Expedite half upfront and half upon delivery of your request**, to encourage him to act even faster.

The following ritual structure and prayer are arranged to accommodate this, but feel free to do what feels the most natural to you.

On other traditions, you can flip your icon of Expedite upside down while he's working to fulfill your request, the idea being that he'll move swiftly in order to get turned right side up again. This is obviously easier to do with an image than a statue and is entirely optional.

Other items at home on Expedite altars include:

- Coins
- Paper money and checks
- A bell or small chime to ring at the start and end of your petitions
- St. Expedite oils, incenses, and perfumes
- Small varieties of palm, bamboo, or plants with red flowers
- Items that are red, green, or gold
- Skeleton keys and lock picks
- Holy water, crosses, rosaries, and other Christian iconography and implements
- Tarot cards and symbols related to your specific (and current) requests
- Dice or playing cards

Timing — St. Expedite + Astrology

In an ideal scenario, it is recommended to set up a new altar dedicated to St. Expedite, or cleanse and reorganize an existing one, on Wednesdays, which is traditionally considered his day, as well as the day associated with the planet Mercury. While most approaches to planetary magic focus primarily on the influence of celestial bodies, it is important to recognize that space weather affects all aspects of life, both positively and negatively. Therefore, incorporating appropriate timing into magical practices can enhance their effectiveness. Ultimately, practical magic is a matter of probabilities.

Since St. Expedite is a spiritual entity, specific timing is not required to work with him. However, if you choose to align your efforts with certain time periods, the results he delivers are likely to be even more favorable. To connect St. Expedite with your planetary magic endeavors, you can associate your requests with the rulers of the houses in your natal chart. By doing so, you can make offerings and offer prayers during those specific periods, further integrating St. Expedite's influence into your magical work.

For example, if your intention is to seek financial abundance and your second house in your natal chart is associated with Pisces, Jupiter is the planet that holds the greatest influence over your financial matters. To enhance the effectiveness of your prayers and offerings, it is advisable to choose either the day of St. Expedite (Wednesday) or the day associated with Jupiter (Thursday) and perform your rituals during the hour ruled by Jupiter.

To provide a quick overview for those unfamiliar with the

correlation between the houses and various aspects of life:

1st House: Pertains to your overall self, including your physical body and personal presentation.

2nd House: Deals with financial matters and material assets.

3rd House: Relates to your daily activities and short-distance travel.

4th House: Represents your household, place of origin, and family.

5th House: Reflects luck, creative endeavors, children, and activities pursued for enjoyment.

6th House: Relates to health, habits, expenses, and pets.

7th House: Involves your spouse, business partners, close one-on-one relationships, and interactions with the external world.

8th House: Pertains to debts and shared resources.

9th House: Deals with higher education, long-distance travel, and religious or philosophical pursuits.

10th House: Relates to your career, public image, and reputation.

11th House: Involves online networks, social groups, communities, and hobbies.

12th House: Represents the subconscious mind and psychological aspects.

Each sign in astrology is ruled by a specific planet:

Aries and Scorpio are ruled by Mars. Taurus and Libra are ruled by Venus. Gemini and Virgo are ruled by Mercury. Cancer is ruled by the Moon. Leo is ruled by the Sun. Sagittarius and Pisces are ruled by Jupiter. Capricorn and Aquarius are ruled by Saturn.

To determine the appropriate planetary hour for your rituals, you can utilize online resources or smartphone applications like Time Nomad, which is available for free on iPhone.

By aligning your prayers and offerings with the relevant planetary influences and utilizing the designated hours, you can further integrate the energies of St. Expedite and the planetary rulers into your spiritual practice.

Forming Your Request

It is crucial to be specific and precise when formulating your petitions and prayers. Take the time to contemplate and clearly define your needs and desires, and consider writing them down to be read during your ritual. The way you phrase your requests plays a significant role in effective communication with all beings involved and can greatly influence the manifestation of your desired outcomes. Here are some fundamental considerations:

- Clearly state your ultimate objective, providing a clear and concise description of what you are seeking to achieve.
- Identify any individuals or parties who are involved in your request, including their full names or specific titles. For example, if you are aiming for a promotion at your current job, mention the name of your manager or the person responsible for making that decision. If you are seeking employment in general, you could phrase it as "Prompt my future boss to hire me immediately and allow me to start working without delay!"
- Specify the setting or location where you wish for the desired outcome to occur. If applicable, mention the exact address or venue. For instance, if you are trying to sell your house, you might say something like "Facilitate

the immediate sale of my house at 123 Expedite Way in California! Ensure that I receive multiple offers exceeding the asking price and expedite the closing process. Promptly transfer the funds from the sale into my account!

- What is the desired time frame for achieving this? In general, it is advisable to request that your needs be fulfilled "today!", "immediately!", "as soon as possible!", or "without any delay!" even if there is a deadline set for the future. St. Expedite is known to be responsive to urgent situations, so even if your request is more of a desire than an immediate necessity, it is effective to emphasize the need for swift action and demand speedy results.

- What is the reason behind your need? To further enhance your petition, you may choose to provide reasons to St. Expedite that explain why the requested outcome is crucial, adding emotional weight and a sense of urgency. For instance, you could state, "I urgently require $2,000 to pay my rent and ensure that my family has a roof over their heads and enough food to eat!" However, it is important to strike a balance and not dwell excessively on the negative aspects of your situation. Be mindful of your phrasing to avoid magnifying difficulties or reinforcing negative circumstances.

General Petition + Prayer to St. Expedite

Prepare your offerings and have your request ready by the altar. You can add your own request and print the script that follows below the prayer text. Additionally, you can compose your own or search through hundreds of additional St. Expediency petitions that are available online.

You ought to be able to utter the Latin term "HODIE," which signifies Expedite's cross and meaning "today" or "at the present time." It is pronounced with the ghost of a (h): (h)o•dee•aay.

Listen —

Give passionate prayers and sacrifices, and speak to the spirit as if it were standing there in front of you, much as you would give a gift and converse with someone you have great respect, reverence, and admiration for. Start by lighting the candle(s) and any incense that you plan to use. Here is a sample petition text:

Oh Saint Expedite, Saint Expedite, Saint Expedite! [Ring the bell or knock three times on the altar] I summon you, here and now, and beseech your intervention! You who act swiftly and reliably in times of need! Clothed in the vibrant colors of a Roman centurion, Holding high your sacred cross inscribed with the word "HODIE"! Carrying a palm frond, symbolizing the triumph of Spirit over matter, Expedite, who heard the crow proclaim "tomorrow", Expedite, who rejected the beast and boldly proclaimed "TODAY"! Come to my aid, illustrious martyr! Grant me this, my prayer and request — [Express your desires; place your petitions or symbols] I offer you... [place them on the altar if not already there, and speak aloud: a flame, water, a poundcake, flowers, and...] In gratitude for your unwavering service and upon the fulfillment of these needs, I will present you with additional offerings and sing your praises to the heavens, For all should bear witness to your power and magnificence! Expedite, Leader of the Thundering Legions, Through the splendor and grace of your Divine Providence, Find a way. Go forth and make it so! This very moment! HODIE, HODIE, HODIE! Amen!

Upon Receipt of Requests, and Disposal of Offerings

Regarding the offerings you make while waiting for your requests to be fulfilled, you can leave them on the altar for as long as you wish, but be sure to remove them before they spoil or wither. As for the water used for offerings, if you have house plants, especially palms, it is beneficial to water them with it (more details on specific applications below). For other offerings, you can place them outside for animals to consume or allow them to decompose as compost.

Once you have received the results you asked for, it is important to return to St. Expedite's altar and fulfill the further offerings and expressions of gratitude that you promised (if any). This can be as simple as placing the offerings on the altar and sincerely saying, "thank you" to St. Expedite from the depths of your heart.

St. Expedite appreciates public recognition. It is customary to sing his praises and share information about him after he has granted your requests. One way to offer recognition is by posting pictures, praises, and relevant hashtags on social media. Alternatively, you can choose to share your experiences and spread the word about St. Expedite in person. In some South American countries, it is common for people to distribute prayer cards on the streets by the hundreds as a way of offering thanks and spreading awareness about St. Expedite's intercessory power.

Formulas for oils, incenses, powders, and washes for use in St. Expedite conjure and devotion

Oils, incense, powders, and washes are commonly used in spiritual practices to enhance the connection with saints and facilitate the manifestation of desired outcomes. These preparations, when properly crafted and used with focused intent, can amplify the energy and intention of your prayers and rituals dedicated to St. Expedite. Here are some traditional formulas for oils, incenses, powders, and washes that you can incorporate into your St. Expedite conjure and devotion:

Blessing and Consecration Ritual:

- Gather the ingredients for your chosen formula.
- Set up a sacred space with candles, a picture or statue of St. Expedite, and any other items that hold personal significance.
- Begin with a prayer, invoking the presence and blessings of St. Expedite.
- Light the candles and focus your intention on the items

you're about to create.

- Follow the specific instructions for each formula (oil, incense, powder, or wash) while reciting prayers or affirmations, infusing them with your intentions and devotion to St. Expedite.
- As you mix the ingredients, visualize the energy of St. Expedite infusing them, imbuing them with his power and assistance.
- Offer a prayer of gratitude and ask for St. Expedite's blessings upon the finished product.
- Place the item on your St. Expedite altar or in a dedicated space, and ask for his continued guidance and support.

Oil Production and Blessing:

- Choose a carrier oil such as almond oil or olive oil as your base.
- Add specific essential oils corresponding to your intention (e.g., rose for love, cinnamon for fast results).
- Combine the oils while reciting a prayer or invocation to St. Expedite, asking for his blessing and assistance.
- Hold the bottle of oil in your hands, visualize it being filled with divine energy, and say a prayer to consecrate it for St. Expedite's use.
- Label the bottle with the purpose of the oil and the date it was created.

Incense Production and Blessing:

- Blend resin or powdered herbs corresponding to your intention (e.g., frankincense for protection, cinnamon for success).
- As you mix the ingredients, focus your thoughts on St. Expedite and his ability to swiftly manifest your desires.
- Burn a small portion of the incense on charcoal and let the smoke carry your prayers and intentions to St. Expedite.
- Recite a prayer of consecration, dedicating the incense to St. Expedite and asking for his assistance.

Powder Production and Blessing:

- Combine powdered herbs, resins, and other ingredients that align with your intention (e.g., sea salt for purification, cinnamon for speed).
- As you mix the ingredients, envision St. Expedite's energy permeating the powder and activating its magical properties.
- Transfer the powder into a container while reciting a prayer or invocation, consecrating it for St. Expedite's use.

Wash Production and Blessing:

- Prepare a base for your wash, such as water or holy water.
- Add cleansing or empowering ingredients like lemon juice, herbs, or essential oils.
- Stir the mixture clockwise while focusing on your intention and asking for St. Expedite's blessings.
- Recite a prayer of consecration, declaring the wash a tool

for spiritual cleansing and empowerment.

Remember, during the production and blessing process, to maintain a state of reverence and focus on your connection with St. Expedite. Trust in his intercession and the power of these magical items to enhance your devotion and manifest your desires.

Novena Prayer: Prayer that Never Fails

Act of Contrition:

The Act of Contrition is a prayer of repentance and sorrow for our sins. It expresses our regret for having offended God, acknowledges the consequences of sin, and declares our firm resolve to seek forgiveness, make amends, and strive for a better life in accordance with God's will. It is often recited during the Sacrament of Reconciliation (Confession) as an essential part of seeking God's mercy and forgiveness.

"Oh my God, I am heartily sorry for having offended you, and I detest all my sins because I dread the loss of heaven and the pains of hell, but most of all because they offend you, my God, who are all good and deserving of all my love. I firmly resolve, with the help of your grace, to confess my sins, to do penance, and to amend my life. Amen."

Day 1:
(Say the Act of Contrition...)

O St. Expedite, you who are always ready to help those in need, we come before you today seeking your intercession. Please hear our prayers and grant us your swift assistance. We humbly ask for [state your intention]. St. Expedite, we trust in your powerful intercession, and we place our hope in your aid. Please come to our aid and help us in our time of need. Amen.

(Now pledge to offer Saint Expedite a specific gift when your desire is fulfilled.) Amen. Recite 1: Our Father... Recite 1: Hail Mary... Recite 1: Glory Be...

Day 2:

(Say the Act of Contrition...)

O Glorious St. Expedite, you who are known for your speedy assistance, we turn to you again with fervent hearts. We ask for your intercession in obtaining [state your intention]. Please pray for us and present our petitions before the throne of God. We trust in your intercession and ask for your quick response. St. Expedite, please come to our aid and help us in our time of need. Amen.

(Now pledge to offer Saint Expedite a specific gift when your desire is fulfilled.) Amen. Recite 1: Our Father... Recite 1: Hail Mary... Recite 1: Glory Be...

Day 3:

(Say the Act of Contrition...)

O Faithful St. Expedite, patron of urgent causes, we gather before you once more, seeking your powerful intercession. Please present our requests to our Heavenly Father and ask Him to grant us [state your intention]. We place our trust in your intercession, knowing that you are always ready to assist those who call upon you. St. Expedite, please come to our aid and help us in our time of need. Amen.

(Now pledge to offer Saint Expedite a specific gift when your desire is fulfilled.) Amen. Recite 1: Our Father... Recite 1: Hail

Mary... Recite 1: Glory Be...

Day 4:

(Say the Act of Contrition...)

O Merciful St. Expedite, who never fails to respond to those who seek your aid, we come before you today with grateful hearts. We thank you for your intercession thus far and ask for your continued help in obtaining [state your intention]. We rely on your quick assistance, knowing that you are a powerful advocate. St. Expedite, please come to our aid and help us in our time of need. Amen.

(Now pledge to offer Saint Expedite a specific gift when your desire is fulfilled.) Amen. Recite 1: Our Father... Recite 1: Hail Mary... Recite 1: Glory Be...

Day 5:

(Say the Act of Contrition...)

O Compassionate St. Expedite, you who understand the urgency of our needs, we approach you with unwavering faith. Please intercede for us and obtain from our Lord the fulfillment of our petition for [state your intention]. We believe in your ability to bring about swift resolutions. St. Expedite, please come to our aid and help us in our time of need. Amen.

(Now pledge to offer Saint Expedite a specific gift when your desire is fulfilled.) Amen. Recite 1: Our Father... Recite 1: Hail Mary... Recite 1: Glory Be...

Day 6:

(Say the Act of Contrition...)

O Mighty St. Expedite, patron of desperate cases, we stand before you once again, seeking your powerful intercession.

Hear our prayers and present them before the throne of God. We ask for your assistance in obtaining [state your intention]. We trust in your prompt response and give thanks for your intercession. St. Expedite, please come to our aid and help us in our time of need. Amen.

(Now pledge to offer Saint Expedite a specific gift when your desire is fulfilled.) Amen. Recite 1: Our Father... Recite 1: Hail Mary... Recite 1: Glory Be...

Day 7:

(Say the Act of Contrition...)

O Valiant St. Expedite, you who are renowned for your miraculous help, we approach you with confidence and gratitude. Thank you for your intercession thus far, and we ask for your continued assistance in obtaining [state your intention]. Please present our petitions before our Heavenly Father, and obtain for us a swift resolution. St. Expedite, please come to our aid and help us in our time of need. Amen.

(Now pledge to offer Saint Expedite a specific gift when your desire is fulfilled.) Amen. Recite 1: Our Father... Recite 1: Hail Mary... Recite 1: Glory Be...

Day 8:

(Say the Act of Contrition...)

O Glorious St. Expedite, who always comes to the aid of those who call upon you, we come before you with hope and trust. We ask for your powerful intercession in obtaining [state your intention]. We believe in your ability to obtain swift assistance for us. St. Expedite, please come to our aid and help us in our time of need. Amen.

(Now pledge to offer Saint Expedite a specific gift when your desire is fulfilled.) Amen. Recite 1: Our Father... Recite 1: Hail Mary... Recite 1: Glory Be...

Day 9:

(Say the Act of Contrition...)

O Miraculous St. Expedite, we have reached the final day of this novena, filled with faith and gratitude. We thank you for your intercession and the assistance you have provided thus far. Today, we ask for your continued help in obtaining [state your intention]. As we conclude this novena, we place our complete trust in your intercession, knowing that you are a faithful advocate. We ask that you present our petitions before our Heavenly Father and obtain for us a swift and favorable response. St. Expedite, please come to our aid and help us in our time of need. Amen.

O Glorious St. Expedite, we thank you for your intercession and for the grace and blessings you have bestowed upon us. As we await the fulfillment of our petition, we promise to spread devotion to you and share your miraculous assistance with others. May your name be praised, and may your example of faith and urgency inspire us always. St. Expedite, we place our trust in you, and we give glory and honor to your name. Amen.

(Now pledge to offer Saint Expedite a specific gift when your desire is fulfilled.) Amen. Recite 1: Our Father... Recite 1: Hail Mary... Recite 1: Glory Be...

Note: Feel free to customize the novena by adding specific intentions and personal prayers based on your needs and circumstances.

Saint Expedite Prayer for Urgent Needs

This prayer is to be recited daily until your request is granted. Make sure to share this prayer of gratitude to Saint Expedite, so that his name and glory may be widely known.

Oh, blessed Saint Expedite, patron saint of urgent causes, in this time of pressing need, I turn to you with unwavering faith in my heart. I seek your intercession, recognizing your immense power as an ally in times of trouble.

With the words of the Psalms, I lift my prayers to you, Saint Expedite, blending the wisdom of scripture with the urgency of my needs.

Psalm 40:13-17: "Please, Lord, come to my rescue swiftly! Let those who seek my harm be put to shame and disgrace. Let them be turned back in their wickedness. Let them be appalled by their own shame. But let all who seek you rejoice and be glad in you; let those who love your salvation always say, 'Great is the Lord!' As for me, I am poor and needy, but you, O Lord, have not forgotten me. You are my help and deliverer; do not delay, O my God!"

Saint Expedite, I invoke these words of the psalmist, beseeching your prompt assistance and divine intervention. Come to my aid, O saint of urgent needs, and present my case before our compassionate and merciful God.

Psalm 31:2-3: "Incline your ear to me, come quickly to my rescue! Be my rock of refuge, a fortress of defense to save me. For you are my rock and my fortress; lead me and guide me for the sake of your name."

Saint Expedite, be my rock and refuge in this time of urgency, shielding me from harm and guiding me toward a swift resolution. Advocate for me, O saint of miracles, that I may find solace and deliverance in my hour of need.

Psalm 70:1-2: "Please, God, come to my rescue. O Lord, hurry to help me! Let those who seek my life be put to shame and confusion. Let them be turned back and humiliated, those who desire my downfall."

Through these verses, Saint Expedite, I implore your assistance and protection, so that those who wish me harm may be deterred and perplexed. Grant me deliverance and restoration, O saint of urgent causes, and may your divine intervention swiftly resolve my troubles.

Saint Expedite, I place my trust in your powerful intercession, fully confident that you will bring my urgent needs before the throne of God. In gratitude for your aid, I will promote devotion to your holy name and express gratitude for the blessings bestowed upon me through your assistance.

In the name of the Father, and of the Son, and of the Holy Spirit, Amen.

Remember, as you pray to Saint Expedite or any saint, do so with a sincere and humble heart, trusting in their intercession and the guiding hand of God. May your urgent needs find resolution, and may your faith be strengthened through the grace and assistance of Saint Expedite.

Prayer to St. Expedite for Healing

O beloved Saint Expedite, patron of urgent causes and miraculous healings, I come before you with a heart burdened by illness and in need of healing. You, who have shown your powerful intercession in times of distress, I humbly implore your aid and invoke the healing power of our Lord.

With the soothing words of the Psalms, I lift my prayers to you, St. Expedite, Combining the strength of scripture with the fervency of my supplication.

Psalm 103:2-4: "Bless the Lord, O my soul, and forget not all his benefits, who forgives all your iniquity, who heals all your diseases, who redeems your life from the pit, who crowns you with steadfast love and mercy."

St. Expedite, I invoke these words of praise and healing, Asking for your intercession in my time of physical and emotional distress. May the Lord, in His infinite mercy, forgive my iniquities, And grant me healing from every disease that afflicts me.

Psalm 41:2-3: "The Lord protects and preserves them— they are counted among the blessed in the land— he does not give them over to the desire of their foes. The Lord sustains them on their sickbed and restores them from their bed of illness."

St. Expedite, I beseech you to stand as my protector and

sustainer, Shielding me from harm and restoring me to health. May my enemies be powerless before the healing grace of the Lord, And may I be uplifted from my bed of illness into renewed strength.

Psalm 147:3: "He heals the brokenhearted and binds up their wounds."

St. Expedite, I humbly ask for your intercession in my emotional and spiritual healing, That the wounds of my heart may be bound and mended by God's loving hand. May I experience the comforting presence of the Lord in my time of distress, And find solace and restoration in His divine healing.

With faith and trust in your powerful intercession, St. Expedite, I surrender my healing journey into your hands. Guide me towards the remedies and treatments that will bring healing, And grant me the strength and perseverance to endure this season of illness.

St. Expedite, I offer my gratitude for your unwavering compassion and assistance, And I promise to spread devotion to your name and honor your holy example. May the Lord, through your intercession, bless me with complete healing, And may I be a living testament to His mercy and grace.

In the name of the Father, and of the Son, and of the Holy Spirit, Amen.

As you pray to St. Expedite for healing, remember to approach with sincerity, faith, and humility. Trust in his intercession and in the healing power of our Lord. May your prayers be heard, and may you find comfort, restoration, and complete healing through the grace of St. Expedite.

Prayer to St. Expedite for Love

O glorious Saint Expedite, patron saint of urgent causes and speedy resolutions, I come before you today with a heart longing for love and companionship. You who have shown your intercession in matters of the heart, I humbly implore your aid and invoke the power of God's Word.

With the wisdom and guidance of the Scriptures, I lift my prayers to you, St. Expedite, Combining the timeless truths of the Bible with the depths of my heartfelt desires.

Genesis 2:18: "Then the Lord God said, 'It is not good that the man should be alone; I will make him a helper fit for him.'"

St. Expedite, I invoke this verse, recognizing that God desires companionship and love for His children. In my longing for love, I ask for your intercession to bring a suitable companion into my life. May God, in His perfect timing, bless me with a loving partner who is a true helper and companion.

Proverbs 18:22: "He who finds a wife finds a good thing and obtains favor from the Lord."

St. Expedite, I turn to you in my quest for love and marriage, Seeking your intercession for the favor of the Lord in finding a life partner. Guide me towards a person who will bring joy, love, and support into my life, And may this union be blessed by God's favor and abundant grace.

1 Corinthians 13:4-7: "Love is patient and kind; love does not envy or boast; it is not arrogant or rude. It does not insist on its own way; it is not irritable or resentful; it does not rejoice at wrongdoing, but rejoices with the truth. Love bears all things, believes all things, hopes all things, endures all things."

St. Expedite, I pray that the love I seek be grounded in the virtues described in this passage. May it be patient, kind, selfless, and enduring, guided by the truths of God's Word. Through your intercession, St. Expedite, may I find a love that brings me closer to God, A love that bears all things, believes all things, hopes all things, and endures all things.

Hebrews 13:4: "Let marriage be held in honor among all, and let the marriage bed be undefiled, for God will judge the sexually immoral and adulterous."

St. Expedite, I ask for your intercession to uphold the sanctity and honor of marriage. May my future relationship be built on a solid foundation of commitment and fidelity, And may it bring glory to God through its purity and faithfulness.

St. Expedite, I place my trust in your powerful intercession, Confident that you will present my prayers before the throne of God. Guide me, protect me, and bless me in matters of love, And may I find joy and fulfillment in a loving relationship that is in accordance with God's will.

In the name of the Father, and of the Son, and of the Holy Spirit, Amen.

As you pray to St. Expedite for love, remember to approach with sincerity, faith, and patience. Trust in his intercession and in God's perfect timing. May your prayers be heard, and may you be blessed with a loving and fulfilling relationship according to God's will and purpose.

Prayer to St. Expedite for Relationship

O blessed Saint Expedite, patron of urgent causes and speedy resolutions, I come before you with a longing heart, seeking your intercession in matters of relationships. You who have shown your powerful aid in times of need, I humbly implore your assistance and invoke the wisdom of God's Word.

With the guidance of Holy Scriptures, I lift my prayers to you, St. Expedite, Combining the eternal truths of the Bible with the depths of my heartfelt desires.

Genesis 2:18: "Then the Lord God said, 'It is not good that the man should be alone; I will make him a helper fit for him.'"

St. Expedite, I invoke this verse, recognizing that God desires companionship and unity for His children. In my pursuit of a meaningful relationship, I ask for your intercession to bring a compatible partner into my life. May God, in His divine plan, bless me with a loving and supportive companion who is a fitting helper.

Proverbs 3:5-6: "Trust in the Lord with all your heart, and do not lean on your own understanding. In all your ways acknowledge him, and he will make straight your paths."

St. Expedite, I turn to you with trust and surrender, seeking divine guidance and discernment. Through your intercession, may I be led to a relationship that aligns with God's will and purpose. Grant me the wisdom to trust in the Lord, to seek His direction in all things, And may He make my path straight and clear in matters of the heart.

1 Corinthians 13:4-7: "Love is patient and kind; love does not envy or boast; it is not arrogant or rude. It does not insist on its own way; it is not irritable or resentful; it does not rejoice at wrongdoing, but rejoices with the truth. Love bears all things, believes all things, hopes all things, endures all things."

St. Expedite, I pray that the relationship I seek be founded on the principles of love described in this passage. May it be characterized by patience, kindness, humility, and selflessness. Through your intercession, may I find a love that rejoices in truth, bears all things, believes all things, hopes all things, and endures all things.

Colossians 3:14: "And above all these put on love, which binds everything together in perfect harmony."

St. Expedite, I ask for your intercession in cultivating a relationship rooted in love. May love be the foundation that binds together every aspect of the relationship, Bringing about harmony, understanding, and unity between myself and my partner.

St. Expedite, I trust in your powerful intercession and in the loving providence of God. Guide me, protect me, and bless me in matters of relationship, And may I find fulfillment and happiness in a relationship that honors God and brings joy to both parties.

In the name of the Father, and of the Son, and of the Holy Spirit, Amen.

As you pray to St. Expedite for a relationship, approach with sincerity, faith, and patience. Trust in his intercession and in the perfect timing of God's plan. May your prayers be heard, and may you be blessed with a relationship that is in accordance with God's will, bringing love, joy, and mutual growth.

.

Prayer to St. Expedite for Miracle

O mighty Saint Expedite, renowned patron of urgent causes and miracles, I come before you with a humble heart, seeking your intercession and divine assistance. You who have shown countless times your miraculous power and swift aid, I implore your intervention and invoke the power of the Psalms.

With the words of the Psalms, I lift my prayers to you, St. Expedite, Combining the timeless praises and supplications with the depths of my urgent needs.

Psalm 34:17: "When the righteous cry for help, the Lord hears and delivers them out of all their troubles."

St. Expedite, I invoke this verse, recognizing that the Lord hears the cries of the righteous. In my time of desperation, I fervently seek your intercession for a miraculous intervention. May the Lord, through your powerful intercession, deliver me from my troubles and grant me the miracle I seek.

Psalm 77:14: "You are the God who works wonders; you have made known your might among the peoples."

St. Expedite, I turn to you as the patron saint of miracles, knowing that you have witnessed the mighty works of God. With your aid, I beseech the Lord to manifest His miraculous power in my life. May He reveal His might and perform a wondrous miracle that will bring about the resolution I need.

Psalm 86:7: "In the day of my trouble I call upon you, for you answer me."

St. Expedite, I call upon you in my time of trouble, trusting in your intercession and your readiness to answer those in need. I lay before you my urgent request, hoping for a miraculous answer and divine intervention. May your prayers on my behalf reach the ears of God, and may He graciously respond to my plea.

Psalm 118:17: "I shall not die, but I shall live, and recount the deeds of the Lord."

St. Expedite, I hold onto the promise of this verse, declaring that I shall not be defeated by my circumstances. With your powerful intercession, may the Lord grant me renewed life and an opportunity to testify to His miraculous deeds. May I witness the manifestation of His power and give glory to His name through the miracle I seek.

St. Expedite, I place my complete trust in your intercession, knowing that you are a saint of quick resolutions. I believe in your miraculous power and the favor you have with our Lord. Guide me, protect me, and intercede on my behalf, So that I may witness the extraordinary intervention of God in my life.

In the name of the Father, and of the Son, and of the Holy Spirit, Amen.

As you pray to St. Expedite for a miracle, approach with unwavering faith and trust in his intercession. Allow the Psalms to inspire and guide your prayers, knowing that God's Word is powerful and effective. May your plea for a miracle be heard, and may you experience the wondrous works of the Lord through the intercession of St. Expedite.

Prayer to St. Expedite for Court Case

O blessed St. Expedite, patron of urgent causes and swift resolutions, I come before you with a heavy heart, seeking your intercession in my court case. You, who have shown your powerful aid in times of need, I implore your assistance and invoke the wisdom of God's Word.

With the guidance of Holy Scriptures, I lift my prayers to you, St. Expedite, Combining the eternal truths of the Bible with the depths of my plea for justice.

Psalm 82:3-4: "Defend the weak and the fatherless; uphold the cause of the poor and the oppressed. Rescue the weak and the needy; deliver them from the hand of the wicked."

St. Expedite, I invoke this verse, recognizing the Lord's call to defend the weak and uphold justice. In my court case, I humbly ask for your intercession to defend my cause and ensure fairness. May you stand with me in the face of injustice, working for the protection and deliverance of the weak and oppressed.

Psalm 43:1: "Vindicate me, my God, and plead my cause against an unfaithful nation. Rescue me from those who are deceitful and wicked."

St. Expedite, I turn to you with a plea for vindication and the pleading of my cause. In this court case, I seek justice against those who act deceitfully and wickedly. With your powerful intercession, may God intervene on my behalf, exposing the truth and bringing forth a just resolution.

Proverbs 21:15: "When justice is done, it brings joy to the righteous but terror to evildoers."

St. Expedite, I pray for the manifestation of true justice in my court case. May the righteousness of my cause bring joy to those who seek the truth and uphold justice. May the evildoers who stand against me be filled with terror as their schemes are unveiled and justice is served.

Psalm 37:5: "Commit your way to the LORD; trust in him and he will do this: He will make your righteous reward shine like the dawn, your vindication like the noonday sun."

St. Expedite, I commit my case into the hands of the Lord, trusting in His divine providence. I seek your intercession to align my path with God's will and His righteous plan. May He make my righteous reward shine like the dawn and bring forth my vindication like the noonday sun.

St. Expedite, I implore your powerful intercession in my court case. Guide my legal team, enlighten the judge, and influence the outcome in accordance with justice. Stand with me as I face the challenges ahead, and may the truth prevail.

In the name of the Father, and of the Son, and of the Holy Spirit, Amen.

As you pray to St. Expedite for your court case, approach with faith, trust, and a sincere desire for justice. Let the Bible verses inspire and guide your prayers, knowing that God's Word holds wisdom and power. May your plea for justice be heard, and may St. Expedite intercede on your behalf to bring about a fair and just resolution to your court case.

Prayer to St. Expedite for Job

O mighty St. Expedite, patron of urgent causes and swift resolutions, I come before you today seeking your intercession in finding meaningful employment. You, who have shown countless times your miraculous aid in times of need, I implore your assistance and invoke the power of the Psalms.

With the words of the Psalms, I lift my prayers to you, St. Expedite, Combining the timeless praises and supplications with the depths of my plea for employment.

Psalm 37:5: "Commit your way to the Lord; trust in him, and he will act."

St. Expedite, I invoke this verse, recognizing the Lord's promise to act when we trust in Him. In my search for employment, I commit my way to the Lord and place my trust in His divine providence. May you intercede on my behalf, St. Expedite, and help me find a job that aligns with my skills, talents, and needs.

Psalm 90:17: "Let the favor of the Lord our God be upon us, and establish the work of our hands upon us; yes, establish the work of our hands!"

St. Expedite, I turn to you, asking for the favor of the Lord to be upon me in my job search. May God establish the work of my hands and guide me towards a fulfilling and prosperous employment opportunity. Through your powerful intercession, may doors open, and opportunities present themselves, leading me to the right job.

Psalm 118:25: "Save us, we pray, O Lord! O Lord, we pray, give us success!"

St. Expedite, I echo this plea, asking for salvation and success in my job search. I beseech your intercession, St. Expedite, to present my prayers to the Lord on my behalf. May the Lord hear my plea and grant me success in securing employment that meets my financial needs and brings fulfillment to my life.

Psalm 127:2: "It is in vain that you rise up early and go late to rest, eating the bread of anxious toil; for he gives to his beloved sleep."

St. Expedite, I bring before you my worries, anxieties, and restless nights in my search for a job. I trust in the promise of this verse that God provides for His beloved. May you intercede for me, St. Expedite, that I may find rest from my anxious toil and experience the divine provision of a job that brings security and peace.

St. Expedite, I seek your powerful intercession and assistance in finding meaningful employment. Guide my steps, open doors of opportunity, and bring forth the right job that aligns with my skills and aspirations. I trust in your swift aid and the favor you have with our Lord.

In the name of the Father, and of the Son, and of the Holy Spirit, Amen.

As you pray to St. Expedite for a job, approach with faith, trust, and perseverance. Let the Psalms inspire and guide your prayers, knowing that they hold the timeless words of praise and supplication. May St. Expedite intercede on your behalf and help you find a job that brings fulfillment, prosperity, and stability in your life.

Prayer to St. Expedite for Money

O mighty St. Expedite, patron of urgent causes and swift resolutions, I come before you today seeking your intercession in matters of financial need. You, who have shown countless times your miraculous aid in times of urgency, I implore your assistance and invoke the power of the Word of God.

With the strength of the Holy Scriptures, I lift my prayers to you, St. Expedite, Combining the timeless promises and teachings with the depths of my plea for financial blessings.

Philippians 4:19: "And my God will supply every need of yours according to his riches in glory in Christ Jesus."

St. Expedite, I invoke this powerful verse, recognizing God's promise to provide for all our needs. In my time of financial struggle, I turn to you for intercession, knowing that you have a special place in the eyes of the Lord. May you present my request before God, and may He, in His infinite abundance, supply the financial blessings I require.

Proverbs 3:9-10: "Honor the Lord with your wealth and with the firstfruits of all your produce; then your barns will be filled with plenty, and your vats will be bursting with wine."

St. Expedite, I come before you, acknowledging the importance of honoring the Lord with my finances. I commit to offering my resources and giving back to the Kingdom of

God. Through your intercession, St. Expedite, I pray that my obedience in honoring the Lord will lead to overflowing abundance in my financial circumstances.

Malachi 3:10: "Bring the full tithe into the storehouse, that there may be food in my house. And thereby put me to the test, says the Lord of hosts, if I will not open the windows of heaven for you and pour down for you a blessing until there is no more need."

St. Expedite, I embrace this verse, understanding the significance of faithful giving and trusting in the Lord's promises. I pledge to bring my tithes and offerings, surrendering my financial worries into the hands of the Lord. Through your powerful intercession, St. Expedite, may the windows of heaven be opened, pouring down abundant blessings upon me, removing all financial burdens.

Luke 6:38: "Give, and it will be given to you. Good measure, pressed down, shaken together, running over, will be put into your lap. For with the measure you use it will be measured back to you."

St. Expedite, I embrace the principle of sowing and reaping, understanding the generosity of God's economy. I commit to giving with a cheerful heart, knowing that as I sow seeds of generosity, I shall also reap a bountiful harvest. Through your intercession, St. Expedite, may God multiply my resources and bring forth blessings in abundance.

St. Expedite, I seek your powerful intercession and assistance in matters of financial need. Guide me towards wise financial decisions, open doors of opportunity, and bless the work of my hands. I trust in your swift aid and the favor you have with our Lord.

In the name of the Father, and of the Son, and of the Holy

Spirit, Amen.

As you pray to St. Expedite for financial blessings, approach with faith, trust, and a sincere desire to honor the Lord with your finances. Let the powerful verses of the Bible inspire and guide your prayers, knowing that God's Word holds promises and truths regarding provision and abundance. May St. Expedite intercede on your behalf, presenting your request before God, and may you experience the financial blessings you need in accordance with His will.

Prayer to St. Expedite for Lottery

O mighty St. Expedite, patron of urgent causes and swift resolutions, I come before you today seeking your intercession in matters of the lottery. You, who have shown countless times your miraculous aid in times of need, I implore your assistance and invoke the power of the Psalms.

With the words of the Psalms, I lift my prayers to you, St. Expedite, Combining the timeless praises and supplications with the depths of my plea for success in the lottery.

Psalm 37:4: "Delight yourself in the Lord, and he will give you the desires of your heart."

St. Expedite, I invoke this verse, recognizing the importance of finding delight in the Lord and aligning my desires with His will. As I seek success in the lottery, I commit to finding joy in the Lord and trusting in His divine guidance. May you intercede on my behalf, St. Expedite, and help manifest the desires of my heart in the lottery.

Psalm 121:2: "My help comes from the Lord, who made heaven and earth."

St. Expedite, I turn to you, acknowledging that my help comes from the Lord, the Creator of all things. In my pursuit of success in the lottery, I seek divine assistance and guidance. Through your powerful intercession, may the Lord grant me favor and bless my endeavors in the lottery.

Psalm 118:24: "This is the day that the Lord has made; let us rejoice and be glad in it."

St. Expedite, I approach the lottery with hope and anticipation, knowing that every day is a gift from the Lord. I rejoice in the opportunities that lie before me and ask for your intercession, St. Expedite, to bring forth favorable outcomes. May the day that the lottery results are revealed be a day of joy and celebration for me, as the Lord's blessings manifest.

Psalm 90:17: "Let the favor of the Lord our God be upon us, and establish the work of our hands upon us; yes, establish the work of our hands!"

St. Expedite, I bring before you my desire for financial abundance through the lottery. I seek the favor of the Lord to be upon me, guiding the work of my hands as I participate in the lottery. Through your intercession, St. Expedite, may the work of my hands in purchasing a lottery ticket be established and blessed by the Lord.

St. Expedite, I seek your powerful intercession and assistance in my pursuit of success in the lottery. Guide me towards wise decisions, open doors of opportunity, and bless my endeavors. I trust in your swift aid and the favor you have with our Lord.

In the name of the Father, and of the Son, and of the Holy Spirit, Amen.

As you pray to St. Expedite for success in the lottery, approach with faith, trust, and a humble heart. Let the Psalms inspire and guide your prayers, knowing that they hold the timeless words of praise and supplication. May St. Expedite intercede on your behalf and help manifest favorable outcomes in the lottery, in alignment with God's will.

Litany of St. Expeditus

A Litany is a prayer form structured around a series of petitions, recited or sung by a soloist (usually, a priest) and responded to by one person or a group of people. Litanies can be used to invoke God, His Son Jesus Christ, and many saints (The Virgin Mary, St. Joseph, St. Rita, etc.). Discover the Litany of St. Expeditus, an important figure to Christians all around the world, and to whom many prayers are dedicated.

The Litany of St. Expeditus

"Lord, have mercy on us. Christ, *have mercy on us.*

Lord, *have mercy on us.*

Christ, hear us. Christ, *graciously us.*

God the Father of Heaven, *have mercy on us.*

God the Son, Redeemer of the world, *have mercy on us.*

God the Holy Ghost, *have mercy on us.*

Holy Trinity, one God, *have mercy on us.*

Holy Mary, Queen of martyrs, *pray for us.*

Saint Expeditus, invincible athlete of faith, *pray for us.*

Saint Expeditus, thou who didst stay faithful to the end, *pray for us.*

Saint Expeditus, thou who didst lose all to win Jesus Christ, *pray for us.*

Saint Expeditus, thou who didst submit to be beaten with rods, *pray for us.*

Saint Expeditus, thou who wast slain by the sword, *pray for us.*

Saint Expeditus, thou who didst receive from the Lord the crown of righteousness, which He hath promised to those who love Him, *pray for us.*

Saint Expeditus, Patron of the Youth, *pray for us.*

Saint Expeditus, Help of Scholars, *pray for us.*

Saint Expeditus, Model of Soldiers, *pray for us.*

Saint Expeditus, Protector of Travellers, *pray for us.*

Saint Expeditus, Advocate of Sinners, *pray for us.*

Saint Expeditus, Health of the Sick, *pray for us.*

Saint Expeditus, Consolation of The Afflicted, *pray for us.*

Saint Expeditus, Mediator of Lawsuits, *pray for us.*

Saint Expeditus, our help in urgent matters, *pray for us.*

Saint Expeditus, who dost teach us never to defer, *pray for us*

Saint Expeditus, Most faithful support of those who hope in thee, *pray for us*

Saint Expeditus, whose protection at the hour of death insures salvation, *pray for us.*

Lamb of God, Who takest away the sins of the world, *Spare us, O Lord.*

Lamb of God, Who takest away the sins of the world, *Graciously hear us, O Lord.*

Lamb of God, Who takest away the sins of the world, *Have mercy on us.*

V. Pray for us, O Saint Expeditus,

R/ That we may be made worthy of the promises of Christ.

Let us pray:

Almighty and Eternal God, Who art the consolation of the afflicted and the support of those in pain, deign to receive the cries of our distress, so that by the intercession and merits of thy glorious martyr, St Expeditus, we may joyfully experience in our extreme necessity the help of thy mercy, through Christ Our Lord."

Why Pray The Litany of St. Expedit?

St. Expeditus is the Patron saint of the youth, scholars, and most particularly, of emergencies. You can pray for his help in various situations: conflicts, lawsuits, exams, driving tests… His litany is designed to help us invoke him by naming his many patronages and the important events of his life (his conversion to Christianity, his martyrdom, etc.). St. Expeditus, or Expedite, was a roman centurion of the III century, who was determined to show his faith proudly: he converted without hesitation and testified of his faith to his fellow soldiers. He was flogged and decapitated for refusing to deny his faith in God.

St. Expeditus is known for not procrastinating: we pray to him, that he inspires us to do the same, and that we find quick resolutions for our problems. When praying his litany, we choose to entrust everything to him and his values, which is why we enumerate his many qualities and gifts: to build a form of closeness with the saint, so that he brings our prayers to the Lord.

How to Pray to St. Expeditus

You can always recite the litany of St. Expeditus, ending each verse with "pray for me". However, there are other more specific prayers to St. Expeditus you can recite in for special situations:

Nine Hour Novena to St. Expedite

St. Expedite is a highly esteemed and widely adored saint in New Orleans. He holds the title of patron saint for those seeking swift resolutions to their problems, individuals striving to overcome procrastination and delays, and those pursuing financial success. People also invoke him for prompt solutions to business issues, winning court cases, securing employment, and various other matters. Interestingly, he has recently earned the nickname "Patron Saint of Nerds" due to his association with computer programmers and hackers. It is believed that he grants requests within his power on the condition that the petitioner shares his invocation with others. While St. Expedite has gained popularity among conjure doctors and in the practice of Catholic Conjure, he has long been an integral part of the tradition of folk Catholicism in Louisiana.

In New Orleans Voudou, St. Expedite is closely linked with the lwa (spirit) known as Baron Samedi, who embodies death, guards cemeteries, and oversees the family of ancestral spirits called the Guede. In Haitian Vodou, the lwa Baron La Croix is often associated with St. Expedite. This connection with Baron Samedi makes St. Expedite a favorite among sorcerers, conjure doctors, and those who view him as a potent magician. Although there is limited information available about this aspect of his character in the literature, and scant references to him in the context of Hoodoo, except for the Hyatt texts where he is referred to as the "Saint of Many Colors" and the "Minute Saint." The focus of this article, however, centers on the Nine Hour Novena to St. Expedite, a strictly Catholic practice that aligns well with conjuring.

Much of St. Expedite's life remains shrouded in mystery, as little has been documented aside from his martyrdom and the stories surrounding the discovery of his statue. According to Father Dan Cambria of the Divine Mercy Chapel in New Orleans, one account tells of the Ursuline nuns receiving an unidentified statue just before the French Revolution. The words "Expedite" were prominently displayed all over the crate in which the statue was enclosed. Upon opening the crate, the nuns found a statue whose identity they couldn't discern. They sought the bishop's assistance in identifying the saint, but he was unable to do so. Desperate for answers, the nuns wrote a letter to the senders in France to inquire about the saint's identity. Unfortunately, due to the ongoing French Revolution, they never received a response. As a result, they placed the statue, now known as St. Expedite, in the corridor of their school where it remained for several decades.

Over time, the students at the convent developed what is now known as the Nine Hour Novena to St. Expedite. Novenas, which are nine-day prayers to various saints, are not uncommon in Catholicism. However, St. Expedite's novena involved praying for nine consecutive hours, and according to the story, the students experienced positive outcomes when practicing this swift novena. His devotion continued to grow among the student body, earning him a reputation for delivering rapid results to prayers.

Below are instructions for performing the Nine Hour Novena to St. Expedite, as well as printable images that can be used in your interactions with him.

Nine Hour Novena to St. Expedite

In Catholicism, a novena is a traditional prayer that lasts for nine consecutive days, with the prayer being said at the same time each day. Novenas are commonly used when seeking the intercession of a saint for a specific request, but they can also be offered as prayers of thanksgiving. The Nine Hour Novena to St. Expedite, however, follows a slightly different format. Instead of spanning nine days, it is performed for nine continuous hours, consisting of six Catholic prayers each hour. The novena commences with the Act of Contrition prayer, and each subsequent hour includes a specific prayer for a particular intention, followed by a designated number of Our Fathers, Memorares, and Hail Marys. These individual prayers address various aspects such as faith, hope, strength, detachment, freedom from anger, grace in prayer, purity, and perseverance. At the conclusion of the 9th hour, after all the prayers have been recited, the concluding prayer to St. Expedite is said. The article also includes the standard Catholic prayers at the end for those who may be unfamiliar with them.

It's important to note that the Nine Hour Novena to St. Expedite is particularly effective as a "road opener" novena. If you are facing significant emotional, situational, or conditional obstacles in your life, performing this novena correctly can be highly beneficial.

The Nine Hour Novena is to be recited in the following order:

1. Act of Contrition (to be said at the beginning)
2. A total of fifty-four prayers to Saint Expedite (excluding the Act of Contrition and Closing Prayer), six prayers per hour for nine consecutive hours, along with additional prayers as indicated, followed by the sign of the cross.
3. Concluding Prayer (to be said after all the hourly prayers have been recited), followed by the sign of the cross.

Making the Sign of the Cross For those who may be unfamiliar with the act of making the sign of the cross, it is a gesture of blessing oneself by tracing a cross shape on the body. While performing this gesture, the trinitarian formula is spoken: "In the name of the Father, and the Son, and the Holy Spirit, Amen." This formula can be said aloud or silently. The sign of the cross is typically made using the right hand, with three fingers representing the Holy Trinity (including the thumb). Specific areas of the body may be touched or symbolically touched. The process begins by touching the forehead while saying "In the name of the Father" (In nomine Patris in Latin), then touching the heart area while saying "And the Son" (et Filii), and finally crossing from the left shoulder to the right while saying "And the Holy Spirit" (et Spiritus Sanctus), concluding with "Amen."

Pope Innocent III (1198-1216) stated that we "make the sign of the cross from the left to the right because from misery (left) we must cross over to glory (right), just as Christ crossed over from death to life and from Hades to Paradise."

LET'S BEGIN

Act of Contrition: My Lord Jesus Christ, loving Father, I deeply regret my sins. Please grant me forgiveness for my

63

sins and the grace I seek through the sorrows of Your beloved Mother and the virtues of Your martyr, Saint Expedite.

FIRST HOUR: During the first hour of the novena, it is suggested to pray for the gift of faith.

Glorious Martyr, Saint Expedite, you were blessed with a fervent faith by God Himself. I implore you to awaken the same faith within my heart, that I may wholeheartedly believe in the existence of a benevolent God and, most importantly, be saved from offending Him.

Followed by: Three Our Fathers in honor of the Holy Trinity. One Memorare to the Blessed Virgin Mary. One Hail Mary in honor of Our Lady of Sorrows.

SECOND HOUR: In the second hour of the novena, we pray for the gift of hope, both for ourselves and those who struggle to believe.

Glorious Martyr, Saint Expedite, through the remarkable hope bestowed upon you by God, intercede on behalf of those with wavering belief. Pray that they may receive the rays of hope and be blessed eternally. Also, please beseech God to grant me fervent hope and steadfastness in the face of suffering.

Followed by: Three Our Fathers in honor of the Holy Trinity. One Memorare to the Blessed Virgin Mary. One Hail Mary in honor of Our Lady of Sorrows.

THIRD HOUR: During the third hour of the Novena to Saint Expedite, we pray for liberation from worldly concerns, enabling us to love God more deeply.

My Lord Jesus Christ...

Glorious Martyr, Saint Expedite, through the boundless love

that our Lord instilled in your heart, please release me from the worldly attachments that hinder my love for God. Help me to love only God for all eternity. Amen. (Note that this prayer specifically addresses the removal of obstacles.)

Followed by: Three Our Fathers in honor of the Holy Trinity. One Memorare to the Blessed Virgin Mary. One Hail Mary in honor of Our Lady of Sorrows.

FOURTH HOUR: In the fourth hour of the Novena to Saint Expedite, we pray for the strength to bear the burdens of our own passions.

My Lord Jesus Christ...

Glorious Martyr, Saint Expedite, who comprehended the teachings of our Divine Teacher to carry the cross and follow Him, I implore you to ask Him for the grace I need to overcome my own passions.

Followed by: Three Our Fathers in honor of the Holy Trinity. One Memorare to the Blessed Virgin Mary. One Hail Mary in honor of Our Lady of Sorrows.

FIFTH HOUR: During the fifth hour of the Novena to Saint Expedite, we pray for the grace of detachment, although it is a concept often associated with Buddhism, it is still a valuable virtue.

My Lord Jesus Christ...

Glorious Martyr, Saint Expedite, you were abundantly blessed with heavenly graces, enabling you to embody virtues. I beseech you to help me let go of all emotions and attachments that hinder my journey towards Heaven. (Note that this prayer focuses on clearing the path ahead.)

Followed by: Three Our Fathers in honor of the Holy Trinity.

One Memorare to the Blessed Virgin Mary. One Hail Mary in honor of Our Lady of Sorrows.

SIXTH HOUR: During the sixth hour of the Novena to Saint Expedite, we pray for freedom from anger.

My Lord Jesus Christ…

Glorious Martyr, Saint Expedite, through the sufferings and humiliations you endured for the love of God, please grant me this grace, which pleases God greatly. Free me from anger and hardness of heart, which obstruct the path of my soul. (Note that this prayer serves as a road opener, removing emotional obstacles.)

Followed by: Three Our Fathers in honor of the Holy Trinity. One Memorare to the Blessed Virgin Mary. One Hail Mary in honor of Our Lady of Sorrows.

SEVENTH HOUR: During the seventh hour of the Novena to Saint Expedite, we pray for the grace to pray effectively.

My Lord Jesus Christ…

Glorious Martyr, Saint Expedite, you understand that prayer is the key that unlocks the Kingdom of Heaven. Teach me to pray in a manner that is pleasing to Our Lord and His Heart. May I live solely for Him, die solely for Him, and pray solely to Him for all eternity.

Followed by: Three Our Fathers in honor of the Holy Trinity. One Memorare to the Blessed Virgin Mary. One Hail Mary in honor of Our Lady of Sorrows.

EIGHTH HOUR: During the eighth hour of the Novena to Saint Expedite, we pray for purity of heart.

My Lord Jesus Christ…

Glorious Martyr, Saint Expedite, through the pure intentions that guided your thoughts, words, and actions, please let them also guide me in my relentless pursuit of God's glory and the welfare of my fellow human beings. (Note that this is a purifying prayer.)

Followed by: Three Our Fathers in honor of the Holy Trinity. One Memorare to the Blessed Virgin Mary. One Hail Mary in honor of Our Lady of Sorrows.

NINTH HOUR: During the ninth hour of the Novena to Saint Expedite, we pray for the grace of final perseverance.

My Lord Jesus Christ…

Glorious Martyr, Saint Expedite, who was deeply loved by the Queen of Heaven, to whom nothing was denied, I implore you, my advocate, to beseech her, through the sufferings of her Divine Son and her own sorrows, to grant me today the grace I seek. Above all, I ask for the grace to die before committing any mortal sin. Amen. (Note that this prayer appeals to St. Expedite to specifically intercede with Our Lady of Sorrows on our behalf.)

Followed by: Three Our Fathers in honor of the Holy Trinity. One Memorare to the Blessed Virgin Mary. One Hail Mary in honor of Our Lady of Sorrows.

Concluding Prayer (after all hourly prayers are said): Oh Saint Expedite, my protector, I place my hope in you, trusting that my petitions will be granted if they are for my own good. Please intercede for me before Our Lord, through the intercession of the Blessed Virgin Mary, seeking

Please pay attention to the important condition mentioned in the concluding prayer: "if they are for my own

good." This indicates that the Nine Hour Novena to St. Expedite should be used for positive intentions, such as seeking blessings, healing, finding employment, or overcoming debt. It is not intended for nefarious purposes, such as causing harm to an enemy or manipulating someone into loving you. In such cases, one should invoke St. Expedite as Baron Samedi and not through a novena or other conventional Catholic practices.

Standard Catholic Prayer used in the Nine Hour Novena

The Our Father

The Our Father holds the distinction of being the oldest Christian prayer, directly attributed to Jesus Christ himself. It is recorded in Matthew 6:9-13, where Jesus taught his disciples to pray using these words. This prayer, believed to have originated from Christ, is recited in every Mass.

Our Father, who resides in heaven, may Your name be revered. May Your Kingdom come, and may Your will be accomplished on earth as it is in heaven. Grant us our daily sustenance, and forgive us our transgressions as we forgive those who have wronged us. Guide us away from temptation and protect us from evil. Amen.

Memorare to the Blessed Virgin Mary

The Memorare of the Blessed Virgin Mary is widely recognized as one of the most famous prayers dedicated to Mary. Originally, it was a portion of a longer 15th-century prayer known as the "Ad sanctitatis tuae pedes, dulcissima Virgo Maria."

However, by the early 16th century, Catholics began treating the Memorare as an independent prayer. Father Claude Bernard, a French priest who ministered to prisoners and those facing death sentences, ardently promoted this prayer. He attributed the conversion of many criminals to the intercession of the Blessed Virgin Mary, invoked through the Memorare.

Recall, O most compassionate Virgin Mary, that it has never been heard of anyone who sought refuge under your protection, implored your assistance, or sought your intercession and was left unaided. Filled with this confidence, I hasten to you, O Virgin of virgins, my Mother. I come before you, standing as a sinner, full of sorrow. O Mother of the Incarnate Word, do not reject my petitions, but in your mercy, hear and answer me. Amen.

The Hail Mary

Hail Mary, full of grace! the Lord is with thee; blessed art thou among women, and blessed is the fruit of thy womb, Jesus. Holy Mary, Mother of God, pray for us sinners, now and at the hour of our death. Amen.

Final Directions

After you have finished your prayers, let the candle continue to burn until it naturally extinguishes. Keep the altar dedicated to St. Expedite intact until your request is granted. Sometimes, you may witness positive outcomes even before completing the novena. In such cases, it is important to still fulfill the entire novena as intended. Once your prayer is answered, turn St. Expedite's image right side up and express your gratitude by sharing a message of thanks in the comments section below. Dispose of any remaining ritual materials at a crossroads or in the trash.

"I have faith in you, St. Expedite, to assist all those who seek your help in times of urgent need. Glory be to you, St. Expedite."

Final Thoughts

The practice of praying to saints, such as St. Expedite, is deeply rooted in Christian tradition and finds its foundation in biblical teachings. It is a way for believers to seek divine intercession and find comfort in knowing that they are not alone in their struggles. Praying to saints is not about worshiping them but rather recognizing their closeness to God and their ability to intercede on our behalf.

Creating a home Altar to St. Expedite can be a meaningful and tangible expression of devotion. It serves as a sacred space where one can offer prayers, light candles, and display images or statues of the saint. This personal Altar becomes a focal point for connecting with St. Expedite's presence and seeking his assistance in urgent matters.

When working with St. Expedite, it is important to approach him with sincerity and a genuine desire for help. Offering appropriate items on the altar, such as red flowers, a glass of water, and pound cake, can symbolize your devotion and gratitude. Remember to be mindful of the timing, considering St. Expedite's association with astrology and selecting auspicious days to make your requests.

Forming your request to St. Expedite requires clarity and specificity. Whether it is for healing, love, relationships, miracles, court cases, jobs, money, or even the lottery, clearly articulate your intentions and trust that St. Expedite will intercede on your behalf.

In times of urgent need, the Nine Hour Novena to St. Expedite can provide solace and hope. This series of prayers, including the Our Father, the Memorare to the Blessed Virgin Mary, and the Hail Mary, is a powerful spiritual practice that has brought comfort and answered prayers to many faithful believers.

The Litany of St. Expeditus is another form of prayer that holds significance in seeking his intercession. It is a repetitive invocation of St. Expedite's name and qualities, emphasizing his role as the patron saint of urgent matters. Praying the litany can deepen your connection with St. Expedite and strengthen your faith in his assistance.

As you engage in prayer and devotion to St. Expedite, remember to have faith and trust in God's divine plan. Sometimes our requests may not be fulfilled in the way we expect, but remain open to the guidance and wisdom that comes through this spiritual journey.

May the intercession of St. Expedite bring comfort, courage, and swift resolutions to all who turn to him in times of need. Let us approach him with faith, humility, and gratitude, knowing that he stands as a powerful ally in urgent matters.

References

1. Catholic Online. (n.d.). Saints & Angels - St. Expedite. Retrieved from **https://www.catholic.org/saints/saint.php?saint_id=375**
2. John 14:13-14 (New International Version). Bible Gateway. Retrieved from **https://www.biblegateway.com/passage/?search=John+14%3A13-14&version=NIV**
3. Matthew 6:9-13 (New International Version). Bible Gateway. Retrieved from **https://www.biblegateway.com/passage/?search=Matthew+6%3A9-13&version=NIV**
4. Macaluso, J. (2012). Saint Expedite: The Official Guide. NOLA.com. Retrieved from **https://www.nola.com/religion/2012/04/saint_expeditus_the_official_g.html**
5. Praying to Saints. Catholic Answers. Retrieved from **https://www.catholic.com/tract/praying-to-the-saints**
6. Van Auken, A. (2019). Praying to Saints: The Communion of Saints. Theosophical Society in America. Retrieved from **https://www.theosophical.org/publications/1299**
7. The Catholic Company. (n.d.). St. Expedite: Patron of Urgent Causes. Retrieved from **https://www.catholicc**

ompany.com/getfed/st-expedite-patron-urgent-cau ses/
8. Santini, S. (2018). St. Expedite: Prayers, Offerings, and Rituals for Urgent Petitions. Llewellyn Publications.
9. Keating, J. (2016). A History of Devotion to St. Expedite. Association of Independent Readers and Rootworkers. Retrieved from https://readersandrootworkers.org/ wiki/A_History_of_Devotion_to_St._Expedite
10. Gracie, C. (2016). Saint Expedite: Prayers for Urgent Causes. CreateSpace Independent Publishing Platform.
11. Hoodoo Delish. (n.d.). St. Expedite: The Saint of Fast Results. Retrieved from https://www.hoodoodelish.co m/post/st-expedite-the-saint-of-fast-results
12. Griffin, J. (2016). St. Expedite's Prayer Book: Prayers to St. Expedite. CreateSpace Independent Publishing Platform.

Printed in Great Britain
by Amazon